A Practical Guide to Setting Up Your Business

A PRACTICAL GUIDE TO SETTING UP YOUR BUSINESS

© 2016 The Business Pod Limited

A Practical Guide to Setting Up Your Business

A PRACTICAL GUIDE TO SETTING UP YOUR BUSINESS

Brought to you by The Business Pod Limited
Author – Katherine Baines – FCCA, BA Hons

Web: www.business-pod.co.uk
Email: info@business-pod.co.uk

A Practical Guide to Setting Up Your Business

Disclaimer:

This information is provided and sold with the knowledge that the publisher and author do not offer any legal or other professional advice. In the case of a need for any such expertise consult with the appropriate professional. This book does not contain all information available on the subject. This book has not been created to be specific to any individual's or organisations' situation or needs. Every effort has been made to make this book as accurate as possible. However, there may be typographical and or content errors. Therefore, this book should serve only as a general guide and not as the ultimate source of subject information. This book contains information that might be dated and is intended only to educate and entertain. The author and publisher shall have no liability or responsibility to any person or entity regarding any loss or damage incurred, or alleged to have incurred, directly or indirectly, by the information contained in this book. You hereby agree to be bound by this disclaimer.

Please note this book is intended for readers that are UK based, as there are elements discussed and links provided that only relate to UK based businesses and individuals. All link to external website were correct at time of publishing.

All rights reserved. No portion of this book may be reproduced in any form without permission from the publisher, except as permitted by UK copyright law. For permissions contact: info@business-pod.co.uk

A Practical Guide To Setting Up Your Business by Katherine Baines
Published by The Business Pod Limited
www.business-pod.co.uk
© 2016 The Business Pod Limited

A Practical Guide to Setting Up Your Business

CONTENTS

ABOUT THE AUTHOR

1 – INTRODUCTION

2 - GETTING YOUR MINDSET RIGHT

    The entrepreneur mindset

    Why start a business?

    Setting goals

3 - SKILLS AND QUALIFICATIONS

4 - SETTING OUT YOUR BUSINESS IDEA

    What are you going to do?

    Working out your niche

    Market Research

    What is your USP?

    Who is your target customer?

    Testing your idea

5 - BUSINESS SET-UP

    Sole Trader

    Partnership

    Limited Company

    Setting up as a Sole Trader & Partnership

    Accounts & tax for sole traders and partnerships

    Setting up a Limited Company

    How to set up the limited company

    Register the company with HMRC

© 2016 The Business Pod Limited

A Practical Guide to Setting Up Your Business

    Accounts & tax for limited companies

    How to get money out of your business

    VAT

    PAYE

    Setting up a bank account

    Collecting payments

6 - REGULATIONS

    Legal

    Licences, accreditation and qualifications

    Insurance

    Health and safety

    Data Protection

7 - PLANNING YOUR BUSINESS

    Choosing a name

    Creating a tagline or slogan

    Create Your Logo

    Uniform / branded work wear

    Image & branding

8 - SOURCING YOUR PRODUCTS

    Wholesalers

    Exhibitions

    Importing

    Trade organisations

9 - MARKETING

A Practical Guide to Setting Up Your Business

- Creating a marketing plan
- Marketing - ONLINE
  - Creating a website
  - Using Google analytics
  - Google Adwords for advertising
  - Social Media
- Marketing – OFFLINE
  - Business cards
  - Creating a brochure
  - Networking
  - Marketing Summary

10 - SALES

11 - COMMUNICATIONS & TECHNOLOGY
  - Email
  - Business stationery
  - Telephone
  - Computers
  - CRM Systems
  - Mailchimp
  - Skype

12 - EQUIPMENT

13 - PREMISES

14 - PRICING
  - Pricing

A Practical Guide to Setting Up Your Business

- Service based business
- Product based business
- Summary of breakeven analysis
- Other pricing considerations

15 - ACCOUNTING

- Record keeping
- How to keep records
- Preparing accounts
- Allowable expenses
- Cash flow management

16 - FUNDING

17 - FURTHER ADVICE AND SUPPORT

- Further advice
- Support

18 - SUMMARY FOR SUCCESS

A Practical Guide to Setting Up Your Business

ABOUT THE AUTHOR

Katherine Baines is a Chartered Certified Accountant who has helped many start-up businesses over the last 10 years. Having had a career in retail management before becoming an accountant she has significant experience working with a wide variety of businesses and has a passion for passing on her knowledge to help clients become more successful.

A Practical Guide to Setting Up Your Business

1 – INTRODUCTION

Welcome, and thank you for buying a copy of my first book. I hope you will find it extremely useful and informative.

The reason I have put pen to paper is because I am regularly asked about the best way to set up a business, should you be a sole trader or limited company, how do you register for self-assessment with HMRC?, Do I need a business plan?, How do you get your first customers?, What marketing works? etc. and this book aims to cover all the basics that you need to consider when setting up your business.

Having had a career in retail management before becoming an accountant and then setting up my own accountancy practice in 2013 I have significant experience in general business management and systems, online and offline marketing, and finance.

Throughout the book I will cover all the main aspects you need to consider when setting up a business, and give you my help and advice to help make your journey into self-employment as easy as possible. Please note though that the resources I make reference to here are just things that I have used and come across along my business journey, there is no right or wrong answer to anything and there will always be other numerous options available to you.

Taking the leap of faith to become self-employed is probably one of the biggest decisions you will ever make in your lifetime, however if you plan right and take my advice before taking the plunge I am sure it will be a decision you won't regret.

It will be hard work but if you believe in your idea and never give up you should see the benefits. If you hit a rough patch try to think

A Practical Guide to Setting Up Your Business

outside the box and look for alternative options. Your hard work WILL pay off, but just be mindful sometimes things take a little time to build up before they start to progress in the right direction. Try to aim for steady consistent growth as this will help you and your business develop successfully without too much strain on your resources, financially, emotionally and physically, as setting up any business is very hard work, and you need to have a clear mind to be productive so that you can achieve your goals.

© 2016 The Business Pod Limited

2 - GETTING YOUR MINDSET RIGHT

The entrepreneur mindset
The first thing to consider before you even get in to the nitty-gritty of what you want to do, is make sure you have the right mindset, and the right WHY. What do I mean by this? Starting a business for yourself will be hard work, no matter how expertly you plan there will be curve balls along the way that throw you off course, and you will have times when you start to question yourself as to why you are doing what you are doing. Most start up businesses are just you, on your own, so you don't have any employees or colleagues to whom you can bounce ideas with, and no one to delegate things to that you don't fancy doing yourself, but if you have a determined nature and stay committed to the cause I am confident your business will flourish.

Someone once said to me being interested is very different to being committed, you may have an interest in say mountaineering, and regularly climb UK fells however if you are going to climb Mount Everest you need real commitment to achieve your goal of reaching your peak.

I think of starting a business as a marriage, you are committing yourself to the business 100%; you need to do whatever it takes to make it work.

However remember the key is that from day one you need to create a business that will give you the work life balance you want. There will be occasions where your business comes first as at the end of the day you will be the only one accountable for making things happen, but you must start out the way you mean to go on, otherwise you are likely to become a busy fool and find yourself

A Practical Guide to Setting Up Your Business

achieving less and less, but working more and more hours. I am not trying to scare you here, I just want to make you realise that the buck stops with you, and you have to be ready for this.

I think the best thing about being self-employed is that you are in control of your own destiny, if you put the work in you will see the results, so when you have to work late to finish something off you know it will be worth it as any financial gain will come to you, any great customer feedback will make you feel good as it was you that made it happen.

Here is my 'Mindset Checklist' for new business owners. Here is a list of attributes that I believe you need to ensure you will be successful:

- ✓ Determination
- ✓ Not afraid of hard work
- ✓ Motivation
- ✓ Ability to stay calm in a crisis
- ✓ Take on responsibility
- ✓ Be Flexible

Why start a business?
The next question to ask yourself is 'WHY' do you want to go into business for yourself?

If your main answer is money, then you may have a rude wakeup call a few months down the line.

You may be very lucky and hopefully everything will go 100% to plan and you will hit every target you set for yourself, however in real life very few things go right to plan, as there are too many variables that are outside of your control, so it is important that you always build

A Practical Guide to Setting Up Your Business

in a contingency as things always cost more than you expect, or take more time than you expect for whatever reason.

You must make sure you are going into business for the right reasons, and not just for the money as there will be times when you are so shattered that no money in the world will make things better. You need to love and have a passion for what you do otherwise you will end up just creating another job for yourself.

Setting goals
I was once told that if you want to have a business with a turnover of £100,000 then you need to act like one with a £250,000 turnover, if you want a £500,000 turnover business then you act like a £1m one. And I think there is some truth in this statement. The perception of your business to potential customers needs to exceed the expectations of what the client thinks you will be able to deliver, and that is where branding and the perceived indifference to your competitors comes in to play. You have to set yourself out from the crowd.

It is also important to set yourself goals. As they say if you measure it, you can manage it. So even though it is likely to only be you in the business to start with, it is still important to measure and manage what you do and set yourself goals. If you write your goals down you are more likely to achieve them, and always stretch yourself, for example if you think you can get 5 customers in one month, then give you self a goal of getting 7 customers in one month, this will then get you in the mindset of achieving that bit extra, however it is not too high a goal that it is unattainable.

I suspect you will have heard this analogy before and that is your goals need to be SMART if they are going to work for you. SMART stands for:

A Practical Guide to Setting Up Your Business

- ✓ Specific
- ✓ Measurable
- ✓ Attainable
- ✓ Realistic
- ✓ Timely

© 2016 The Business Pod Limited

3 - SKILLS AND QUALIFICATIONS

And finally before I start helping you plan your business, ask yourself do you have all the skills you need to be successful. There are general skills that you need to become great at when going into business for yourself, they include:

- Sales & marketing
- Customer relationship management
- Organisation
- Communication
- Negotiation
- Bookkeeping & Accountancy
- Leadership
- IT skills

The other element to think about with regard to skills is do you have the skills and expertise to be able to be successful in the business you are going to start? Or do you need further training? Whilst for many businesses you will not need any formal qualifications it is important to know that you have all the skills you need. If you are going to be working in a regulated industry such as accountancy, do you have the necessary practicing certificates to get the insurance you need? Make sure you have done thorough research in your industry to ensure you are aware of any regulations you need to comply with. If there are areas of skill sets that are missing then it is these areas that you would tend to recruit people into.

4 - SETTING OUT YOUR BUSINESS IDEA

What are you going to do?
Due to the fact you are reading this book it suggests you probably already have an initial idea of what you aim to do in your business, however I suspect at this stage your idea may still need to be put down on paper and polished up somewhat.

One way to really define what you are going to do is create a brainstorm of all your ideas for your business, once you have completed this, review it and choose the main items you are going to concentrate on initially. Remember you won't be able to do everything that you'd like to do straight away and you need to concentrate on a few key areas to start with as this will help you with your marketing message and materials to get you up and running.

When defining your products and services don't be afraid to write down everything you think you may want to do, even if you think it is an off the wall idea at the moment because 3-6 months down the line it may not be as off the wall as you think.

As with any business you need to start somewhere, and that is why a brainstorm of your ideas is a great idea to help you then choose 1-3 main areas that you are going to concentrate on initially.

Working out your niche
Businesses that have a niche firstly earn more money and secondly find it easier to market themselves as they have a much defined target market to aim for.

A Practical Guide to Setting Up Your Business

Think about your business idea, who are you helping? who is your target customer?, what do they look like?. Now can you narrow this down any further e.g. Helping people lose weight is a general business idea however specifically helping new mums to lose weight is a niche.

What is a Business Plan? A business plan is an absolute must if you are going to be applying for funding, and by writing down your ideas as you work through this book you will have got the majority of the information you need to put a business plan together. If you don't need a business plan for funding then you can still put one together and use it as a working document to help you consolidate and stay focused on your idea.

Market Research
After making sure you are going in to business for the right reasons you need to make sure that your idea is viable and therefore you need to do some preliminary research. Research is so much easier nowadays than it used to be due to access to the Internet. You can use search engines to find out things like:
- Market reach (How large is your potential market?)
- Is your target market easily within your reach?
- What are the trends? (Are you in an industry that continues to grow?)
- Who are your main competitors (In the local area and UK wide?)
- What are your competitors offering their clients?
- Are there similar products and services already on the market?
- Is your service or product in a niche area?

A Practical Guide to Setting Up Your Business

Another way to do some primary research is to actually get out there and talk to people, for example you could attend a networking group or maybe hold a focus group and ask them what they think of your idea. If you ask people you don't know you are more likely to get an honest answer rather than just asking family members.

The office of National Statistics is also a great place to find some valuable data (www.ons.gov.uk/)

What is your USP?
Once you have done your market research you need to pin point what your USP is. Your USP is your 'unique selling point', it is what sets you out from the competition, and what makes customers choose YOU over someone else offering the same product or service.

It is really important to work out what your USP is, as it will help you when putting your marketing materials together.

Here is an example of a USP is for an accountancy firm. All accountancy firms will offer year end accounts and tax as their main services so what makes one more unique than another? An example could be that they offer fixed fees that can be paid monthly over 12 months, so that the client does not get a large bill that needs to be paid all at once in one big lump sum.

Who is your target customer?
To be able to put effective marketing campaigns together you need to know exactly who your target customer is:
- What age are they?
- What demographic are they? Or how affluent are they?
- Are they male or female?

A Practical Guide to Setting Up Your Business

- Do they have families?
- Are they businesses? If so what size? What industry?

The idea here is to create an avatar of your target customer, give them a name such as Sarah or John the Managing Director, or the Windsor family, and keep them in mind when putting any marketing campaign together as you need to create marketing content relevant to them.

Testing your idea
If you are 100% confident there is a market for your business then see if you can test the business to see if it will work. If you have a physical product could you try and hire a stall at a local craft fair, or market, and try it over a weekend and see what happens, or maybe you could try and sell your product via Ebay as this is a quick way to get a product to market at a low cost, also using Ebay you will get to see how many people have looked at your item, so even if they did not buy it via Ebay if you have had hundreds of views of your product that suggests there may be a market for it.

If you offer services rather than a product then maybe you could set up a 1 page website for yourself and run a Google ad campaign to see how many potential clients get in contact. If you get a good response then you know your idea is good to go.

I have often been told that in the service world you should try and sell the service before you have created it; otherwise you have potentially wasted your time creating a product or service that you may not be able to sell.

Another way to get a feel for your idea is put a post on Facebook or LinkedIn asking for people's views on what you are going to offer.

A Practical Guide to Setting Up Your Business

This should be a slightly less bias than asking friends and family especially on Linked In as most of your contacts on Linked In will be business acquaintances and so one would hope they would give you honest feedback.

Testing isn't always an option, however if you can do a test of some description and you get good results it stands you in good stead to going on to have a successful business.

A Practical Guide to Setting Up Your Business

5 - BUSINESS SET-UP

So you now have your idea, you've done your market research, you believe it is a viable idea, you know who your target customer is, so now it is time to think about how you are going to run your business.

Business structure
When setting up a business you need to decide what business structure you are going to use. We are only going to cover the main types of structure in this book, which are:
- Sole trader
- Partnership
- Limited Company

There are of course other options such as community interest companies, and LLPs (Limited Liability Partnerships). If the above three options that we are going to cover do not suit you then please seek advice from a professional to advise you further.

Sole Trader
A sole trader is a business of one person that is registered as self-employed with HMRC (www.hmrc.gov.uk). You will need to submit a self-assessment tax return to HMRC each year which declares the income and expenses of the business. Ultimately a sole trader is one business owner in charge of everything.

Partnership
A partnership is a business of two or more people that are in business together, and needs to be registered with HMRC. You will need to submit a partnership tax return each year which declares

the income and expenses of the business and declares what % of the profits are attributable to each partner. Those profits will then need declaring on the individual tax returns for each of the partners. Therefore each partner will need to register with HMRC as being a partner in the business so that HMRC issue each partner with a tax return as well as the partnership. One of the partners will need to be appointed as the lead partner and he/she will be responsible for filing the partnership tax return.

Limited Company

A limited company is a business that is registered with Companies House, (www.companieshouse.gov.uk) there can be as many directors and shareholders as you want there to be. You will normally be the director and the shareholder.

Being a limited company means that anyone can access the Companies House register and see who the directors and shareholders of the company are, this can be useful if you are intending to contract with large corporate companies as they are likely to want to check out who you say you are before signing with you, and if you are a sole trader this is not possible until you have been trading a few years and there are credit reference reports available for your business.

Setting up as a Sole Trader & Partnership

To set up as a sole trader or partnership all you need to do its register with HMRC (www.hmrc.gov.uk) for tax. If you do an internet search for 'register with HMRC as self-employed' it should take you straight to the specific page you need. You will set up a government gateway account which will then allow you to register with HMRC for the taxes that you need. You will need your full

A Practical Guide to Setting Up Your Business

name, address and national insurance number to be able to register.

For a sole trader you just need to register as self-employed. For a partnership you need to register the partnership for a partnership tax return, and each of the partners too.

Accounts & tax for sole traders and partnerships
Both sole traders and partnerships need to submit their tax returns to HMRC by 31st January each year and pay tax accordingly in January each year too. There is no requirement for official accounts to be prepared so in theory you could do them yourself however you do need to prepare your financial records in a manner that you can complete your tax return accordingly so preparing proper accounts and using an accountant is still advisable as your accountant will also be able to advise you and the partnership on any current allowances available.

As a sole trader you will currently pay 20% Tax on profits over your personal allowance, and 9% class 4 National Insurance on profits over the Class 4 National Insurance allowance. There is also Class 2 National Insurance which used to be paid separately but this is now payable through your self-assessment tax return.

As a partner you will pay at the same Tax and National Insurance rates based on your % share of the profits.

If your self-assessment tax bill is more than £1000 you will need to pay 'Payments on Account' in the January and July for the following tax year, this is something you need to consider if it is your first year, for example if your first tax bill works out to be £1000, then your tax bill in the January when you file your first return will be £1500, and then there is another £500 due in the July after. This

A Practical Guide to Setting Up Your Business

then means the following January you only have a balancing figure for the year plus the first payment on account for the next year.

I appreciate this is a bit complicated, so here is a link to HMRC's website that gives further advice re payments on account - www.gov.uk/understand-self-assessment-bill/payments-on-account , I would also advise that in your first year you get your year end accounts prepared as soon as you can after your year end so that you know how much your tax bill will be sooner rather than later in case you need to save up to pay it.

I always advise clients to save about 20% of their sales/income in a savings account so that you always have more than enough to cover any tax liabilities after deducting allowable expenses and personal allowance.

Setting up a Limited Company
When setting up a Limited Company it is important to think about the long term, the reason I say this is because if you intend to issue shares to people other than yourself, then my advice it to set up your company with different share capital types.

When you set up an owner managed limited company, you become a director of the company and you also own 'x' amount of shares so you become a shareholder too. Shareholders are the people that own the company, therefore if there are 100 shares issued and you own all of them you own 100% of the company.

A basic company is normally set up with one class/type of shares and you issue yourself with 1 x or 100 x £1 ordinary shares. My advice is to issue 100 shares, you then pay the company £100 for these shares and this gives the company £100 to open the bank account with.

A Practical Guide to Setting Up Your Business

If however you expect to have other shareholders in the future then my advice is to set the company up with more than one class/type of shares, these being £1 A Shares, £1 B Shares and £1 C shares etc. You would still only issue yourself 100 x £1 A shares, but it means the other share classes are available should you need them.

The benefit of having different classes of shares means that you can give different dividends for each share class/type. For example if you take on a second director and they buy 100 B shares they will now own 50% of the business, because there are now 200 shares in issue and you both own 100 shares each, however if you work in the business 40 hours a week and your co-director works 20 hours a week then their dividends should be less than yours as they have invested less time in the business than you. By having the different class/types of shares it means you can propose different dividend rates for each class of share.

If you only have one class of share if you take £1 in dividends then the other shareholder has to take £1 in dividend too, assuming the shares are equally split, so by having different share types it makes it more flexible for rewarding shareholders in a small company in the most fair way possible.

How to set up the limited company
There are two main options for setting up the limited company, one is to do it yourself, and the other is to use a formation agent. If you decide to do it yourself it will cost approx. £15, if you use a formation agent the price will vary, and often they will package others things in for you, e.g. using their address as your registered office address.

A Practical Guide to Setting Up Your Business

Being a limited company means that you become a director of the company you have duties that you have to comply with as outlined in the Companies Act 2006. You will need to submit abbreviated accounts to Companies House within 9 months of the year end and file an annual return once a year confirming who the directors and shareholders of the company are. Due to the statutory nature of the year end accounts of a limited company you are likely to need to use an accountant for your year end accounts and tax.

Register the company with HMRC

The company will need to file a corporation tax return to HMRC annually, and therefore you need to register the company with HMRC.

If you incorporate your company direct with HMRC at the end of the process it should give you the option to register with HMRC at the same time and it will ask you what your year end will be. Unless you change your year end with Companies House your year end date will be the end of the month in which you incorporate for example if you incorporate on 7th April your year end will be 30th April, or 1st March will be 31st March. You can only change your year end once in a five year period therefore it is worth giving some consideration as to when you want your year end to be and incorporate in the correct month from the start to save you having to change your year end manually with Companies House.

If you use an incorporation agent it is likely they won't register you with HMRC and shortly after the company has been incorporated you will receive a letter from HMRC with telling you how to register with them for corporation tax.

© 2016 The Business Pod Limited

A Practical Guide to Setting Up Your Business

Whichever way you choose you will still need to register with HMRC through the government gateway so that you will be able to see your corporation tax online with HRMC.

When registering for self-assessment as a sole trader, partnership, or for corporation tax HMRC will issue you with a UTR number (this is a Unique Tax reference), you will need this to be able to file your tax return, and if using an accountant, he/she will need this number to be able to file your return.

Accounts & tax for limited companies

A limited company has to file its accounts to Companies House within 9 months of its year end. If the company is classified as a small company it can just submit abbreviated accounts to Companies House, this means only a limited amount of information is put in the public domain about your business. Ultimately abbreviated accounts just contain a balance sheet, so no one can see the turnover of the company, the wages that are taken or details of any dividends taken out.

A corporation tax return needs to be filed within 12 months of the year end, however any tax due is payable 9 months after the year end, it has always seemed weird to me that you have longer to file the return than the accounts and that the tax is due before the return is due, but that is the current regulations. Attached to the corporation tax return you need to give HMRC a copy of your full accounts in iXBRL format with the return this helps them check the tax calculation.

If you choose to be a limited company my advice is that you will need to use an accountant due to the statutory nature of the accounts, and as you will need software to create the files needed to submit to Companies House and HMRC.

© 2016 The Business Pod Limited

A Practical Guide to Setting Up Your Business

The current rate of corporation tax for a small company is 20% however this is due to reduce over the next few years. The corporation tax rates get reviewed and amended in the budget each year by the Chancellor of the Exchequer.

As a director of a limited company you will also need to file a self-assessment personal tax return to HMRC to show your salary and dividends, along with another other income you may have such as interest received, rental income from buy to let properties etc.

How to get money out of your business

As a sole trader and partnership ultimately the money in the business after paying the business's debts is yours to take, as you will pay tax on your profits not on your drawings (the money you take out). You must be mindful of this as you will still need to make sure you have money left to pay your personal tax bill.

As a limited company you can only get money out of the company by salary or dividends. Your salary will need to be declared through your monthly payroll (PAYE – further details below), and any dividends can only be distributed to you if you are also a shareholder (which would normally be the case in an owner managed business), and there are profits in the company. The company pays corporation tax on its profits and any reserves left after paying tax will be available to distribute to the company's shareholders. Tax rates on dividends have changed from 6th April 2016; therefore you will need to seek professional advice on your potential tax liabilities.

A Practical Guide to Setting Up Your Business

VAT

You only need to register for VAT if your sales are over £83,000 (correct as at 6th April 2016. This limit tends to change year on year.

You can choose to register for VAT even if your sales/turnover is below this limit. The reason you may wish to do this is if you plan to work with large corporate organisations who expect you to be VAT registered, or you want to make your company look bigger than it is, as if you are VAT registered people tend to assume you have a turnover of more than £83,000, or you believe your business sales/turnover will go over the £83,000 within 30 days.

There are also various schemes that you can use, such as 'cash basis' rather than 'invoice basis', and also 'flat rate' schemes if your turnover is under a certain limit. The advice for which scheme you should use will vary depending on your business and therefore please speak to an accountant or HMRC direct for further information and to advise you accordingly. If you are in a service based business where you buy very few items, then the flat rat scheme could be beneficial to you, therefore please ask your accountant accordingly.

PAYE

Whether you choose to be a Sole Trader, Partnership or Limited Company, if you need to take on staff you will need to register with HMRC for PAYE as an employer so that you are able to pay your employees. As a director of a limited company you will need to become an 'employee' of the company so that you can pay yourself a salary.

To register as an employer you can do this from the government gateway login that you created when you registered to file a tax return.

A Practical Guide to Setting Up Your Business

As an employer you will need to calculate the wages due to the employee and then deduct tax and national insurance based on the employee's tax code on a weekly or monthly basis. A persons tax code can vary from the standard due to other income, historic tax liabilities etc. There may also be other deductions that HMRC ask you to deduct such as student loan repayments, and also deductions from third parties which are normally called 'Attachment of Earnings' (AOE) this is often for child maintenance payments or council tax arrears.

The tax, national insurance and student loan deductions need to be paid across to HMRC by 22nd of the following month. Deductions for AOE's would normally be paid direct to the third party after the wages have been paid.

You will need to pay 'Employer's National Insurance' for employees earning over a certain limit. As at the time of writing there is an Employers Allowance that means many small businesses do not have any employer's national insurance to pay.

As an employer you will also need to comply with statutory minimum wage requirements. Here is a link to the current rates - www.gov.uk/national-minimum-wage-rates

Running a payroll can be a relatively easy task; it is when you get complications such as strange tax codes and attachment of earnings etc that running payroll can be more complicated. If you have any doubt I suggest you outsource this to your accountant. There are also many online options nowadays too. If you do want to process it yourself I would highly recommend using Moneysoft's payroll manager as it provides you with a cost effective solution, or if you use XERO for your bookkeeping (which we cover later on) then

A Practical Guide to Setting Up Your Business

XERO now offers you a payroll solution too. Here is a link to Moneysoft - www.moneysoft.co.uk/payroll-software/payroll-manager.htm

Another consideration which is happening imminently for most small businesses is the introduction of the workplace pension. This is called auto-enrolment and will involve you deducting pension contributions from your employee's wages and paying it across to a pension provider. The employer will also have to make contributions on behalf of the employee too. More information can be found at www.thepensionsregulator.gov.uk/en/employers

Setting up a bank account
This is likely to be one of the last things you do as often banks will want to see your business plan or at least an overview of what you are going to do before opening an account for you, plus if you go down the limited company route they will need to see your certificate of incorporation to prove the company exists.

In my experience most banks seem to ask for different things to verify who you are, if you do already bank with the bank you choose on a personal level then they will have already verified who you are personally which makes the process slightly easier as banks have to comply with the Anti-Money Laundering Regulations.

When opening a bank account you will need a main current account and a deposit account. The deposit account is so that you can transfer 20%-30% of your 'money in' into this account on a monthly basis so that you have enough available when it is time to pay your tax. I appreciate when you are starting this is easier said than done but if you don't start as you mean to go on you can end up with a large tax bill and not have the funds available to pay it.

A Practical Guide to Setting Up Your Business

All banks have different charging structures for their monthly bank fees, so it is worth shopping around the banks to see which account will give you the best deal.

Collecting payments
PayPal now have a chip and pin facility for you to take card payments which appears to be really cost effective and for recurring payments you could consider GoCardless. An alternative option for recurring payments is to ask the client to set up a standing order, which is fine as long as the amount is not going to change, where by using GoCardless you are in control of the amount you request each month, GoCardless notifies the client of the amount you will be taking just like what happens with normal Direct Debits. Here are links to Paypal - www.paypal.com/uk/webapps/mpp/credit-card-reader , and GoCardless www.gocardless.com for more information.

A Practical Guide to Setting Up Your Business

6 - REGULATIONS

Legal
Legal considerations include do you need terms and conditions of trading to put on your invoices or quotes to customers? Will you be taking on staff? If so you will need employment contracts (which we will cover later). Will you be taking on premises? If so you are likely to have to sign a lease which you potentially need to get looked over by a solicitor.

If you have any doubt about any legal issues I recommend you get professional legal advice as it will be money well spent and could actually save you money in the long term.

Licences, accreditation and qualifications
Some businesses need licences and accreditation before they can start to trade. For example if you are a chartered accountant you need a practicing licence before you can start, if you are a hairdresser or beauty therapist to run a successful business and for insurance purposes you are likely to need to be trained to a certain standard.

For the purpose of this book I do assume you will already have the necessary qualifications, however it is still something to consider, maybe there are additional qualifications that you may need down the line to be able to expand your business, or take it to the next level, and therefore the time and cost of doing the additional qualifications should be taken into account.

With regard to accreditation, consider if there are any organisations that you would want to be associated with that will give you the stamp of approval in your industry? E.g. if you are in the beauty industry would it be useful to be a member of the Beauty Guild? If you are a plumber would it be worth being accredited by Checkatrade?

Be careful though; ask yourself 'Do you need it?' When setting up a small business you have to constantly ask yourself do I need this item? What benefits will it bring me? Will it be worth the money? It is very easy to just spend, spend, spend and sometimes it isn't needed, don't think you need to have 'this' because I should, you should only buy something if you are going to get a tangible benefit or result from it.

Other licence issues could include the need for licences from your local council. If you were going to be a street trader, or market stall holder then you are likely to need a licence. You can find out more about this at www.gov.uk/licence-finder

Insurance
In today's society insurance is a must, we all hope nothing will ever happen that means we need to make a claim but you never know. It is better to be safe than sorry, and if you have appropriate cover then you have nothing to worry about if things do go horribly wrong for you.

Nowadays there are many ways to organise your insurance. If you just need basic Professional Indemnity Cover then you can probably do it online yourself, however make sure you read all the small print. If you have any doubt on the cover you need, then my advice would be to speak to an insurance broker who would be able to advise you accordingly.

Other insurances to consider are, car insurance, if you use your car for business use then you need to insure it so, as if you have an accident and you are on company business you potentially will not be covered. Also consider your house insurance if you are going to

A Practical Guide to Setting Up Your Business

work from home and you will be having people visit you at home, will your home insurance cover for public liability if someone injures themselves on your premises? Or will your business insurance cover you if someone has an accident on your property?

Here is a list of potential insurances that you may need to consider:

- **Professional indemnity insurance**, (also known as PI insurance), is a type of liability cover that is designed to protect you against claims made by clients for loss or damage due to negligent advice or services

- **Public liability insurance** would cover you against the cost of claims made by members of the public for incidents that happen in connection with your business such as personal injuries, death, loss or damage to property

- **Vehicle insurance**, by law if you own a car you need vehicle insurance to be able to use the vehicle, however are you covered for business use? Most vehicle insurance would cover you Full Comprehensive, or Third Party Fire and Theft, however if you are going to be using your vehicle for business use you need to upgrade your policy to include business use accordingly.

- **Buildings and property insurance** will cover the buildings that you are renting or own, this is one to look at if you are going to be leasing premises as to whether it is your responsibility or your landlord to insure the building.

- **Contents & equipment insurance** is cover to protect the contents of your business premises, for example if there is a flood, or fire or burglary and you lose all your equipment.

A Practical Guide to Setting Up Your Business

- **Product liability insurance** will cover you if someone is injured by a faulty product that your business designs, manufactures or supplies.

- **Data protection insurance** is designed to protect businesses that hold, process or collect personal data in case the data gets lost or stolen, either accidentally or maliciously.

- **Goods in transit insurance** would cover you for loss or damage of stock being transported; sometimes this is offered direct by your supplier on a per shipment basis, but check if applicable to your business.

- **Directors' and officers' liability insurance** covers the business' directors for claims made about them for alleged wrongful acts such as breach of duty, error, wrongful trading etc.

- **Employers liability insurance** is a legal requirement for most business in the UK if you employ staff, as it covers the business in the event of an employee getting injured at work

Health and safety
I always advise that you should consider health and safety implications even if it is only you in the business. The HSE (Health and Safety Executive) provides an excellent source of information on all things health and safety. More information can be found at www.hse.gov.uk/simple-health-safety/index.htm

A Practical Guide to Setting Up Your Business

Data Protection

Businesses that deal with customer's personal details may need to register with ICO (Information Commissioner's Office). It will depend on what you do with the data as to whether you need to register. It currently costs £35 to register with them. More information can be found at www.ico.org.uk/for-organisations

7 - PLANNING YOUR BUSINESS

Choosing a name

Deciding on a name is probably one of the most difficult things you will have to do as once you have decided on it everything revolves around it, and it's not easy to change at a later date.

Things to consider are:
- What image do you want to portray?
- Do you want to have a name that says what you do?
- Do you want the name to be unusual so that it is a talking point?
- Could you use your personal name?
- Could you use the initials of your family to create a name?

Once you have come up with your name first check to see if it is available at Companies House, at www.companieshouse.gov.uk, even if you are going to trade as a sole trader or partnership and not a company, if a company registered has the same name that you want to use it may give you issues going forward.

Secondly check the domain name and email address is available. I tend to use www.123-reg.co.uk for my domain names; however there are hundreds of providers out there to choose from. A few others are www.godaddy.com , www.fasthosts.co.uk , and www.names.co.uk . The domain name is the web address that you want to use for example www.123-reg.co.uk is a domain name.

If you need help to create a business name you could always outsource it to someone on Fiverr.com.

A Practical Guide to Setting Up Your Business

Creating a tagline or slogan

Once you have decided on your name, you then need to come up with a tagline. This isn't mandatory however a tagline sums up either what you do or what you stand for. Using your USP can help you here. Here are some examples that have been used by well known businesses to get you thinking about your tagline:

- Aldi- Spend a Little, Live a Lot
- Audi - Vorsprung Durch Technik
- BMW – The ultimate driving machine
- BT – It's good to talk
- Gillette – The best a man can get
- Heinz Baked Beans - Beanz Meanz Heinz
- John Lewis – Never Knowingly Undersold
- L'Oreal – Because You're Worth It
- Mars - A Mars a day helps you work, rest and play
- Nike – Just Do It
- Tesco - Every Little Helps
- Toyota - The car in front is a Toyota

Create Your Logo

Now you have your business name you can create your logo. There are various ways you can do this.
1. Do it yourself (cost = just your time)
2. Get a graphic designer to do one (cost = £40 plus)
3. Subcontract it to someone e.g. on Fiverr or Elance (cost = Less than £40)

It depends on your concept and idea for the business as to how professional you want to go, I have two businesses and for the one logo I created it myself in word using shapes, colours and letters, and then used the snipping tool to turn it in to a jpeg file. Three

A Practical Guide to Setting Up Your Business

years in I am still happy with the logo and at the moment do not want to change it. For my second business I used Fiverr, I gave them a brief of what I wanted and I loved what they had created for me. If you are not creative in the slightest then it may be worth the money to get a graphic designer to do this for you, in my experience graphic designer designed logos always look more professional than something you can create yourself. My advice is, if you have the money in your budget get a graphic designer to do it for you.

Uniform / branded work wear

Consider whether you need uniforms, protective clothing, branded clothing etc. Many of the most successful businesses have branded clothing to help advertise their businesses. When you attend networking events not all of them allow you to have a 1 minute slot to tell people about your business, and likewise at the bigger events you will not be able to speak to everyone so if you have branded shirts or polo shirts then people will still get to subliminally know your brand as they will see your logo/name as you mingle at the events.

Image & branding

With all of your marketing materials, including your website, business cards, and any flyers/brochures you create you must portray a consistent image and brand.

A brand by definition is 'the promotion of a particular product or company by means of advertising and distinctive design'; this is created by always providing a consistent image. An example of this in the extreme is Virgin Airlines, where the cabin crew wear flat black shoes on board a long haul flight to be able to do their job without being in pain, however the moment they step off the plane in to the airport you will see they are always in their red heels!

A Practical Guide to Setting Up Your Business

8 - SOURCING YOUR PRODUCTS

If you are planning a product based business then you will need to source your products. This can be one of the trickiest and possibly time consuming things you will have to do as you will need to get samples before buying to ensure the product is as you expect it to be; there may also be some negotiation too which can be an art form in its own right!

Wholesalers
One of the quickest ways to source your products is to actually go and visit a wholesaler. When buying from wholesalers online be careful, if it sounds too good a deal to be true it probably is, there are many unscrupulous traders or scammers out there, so if buying online then do your research and check them out thoroughly before going ahead, and I would suggest paying by credit card too so that you have some protection if the transaction goes wrong. Also when buying from a wholesaler take care to check out their returns policy especially if buying online where you don't see the product before buying it, as if you are unable to return the products if they don't meet your expectations then you are going to be left with stock you will have to sell to get your money back in order to invest in new stock.

Exhibitions
If your business is based in the home and gift arena (including jewellery), then you will find a fantastic selection of contacts at the UK Spring Fair. This has been an annual event for many years and takes place at the NEC near Birmingham. More information can be found at www.springfair.com

A Practical Guide to Setting Up Your Business

Importing

If you are looking to manufacturer or source products in volume then you may wish to look at importing. Alibaba is now the world's leading platform for global trading. More information can be found at www.alibaba.com. If you are looking to import it is important to get samples before you place large orders, and I would suggest getting professional advice or consider using a sourcing agent, this will also help if there is a language barrier. I believe the Chamber of Commerce is a good source of information with regard to Exporting and Importing.

You also need to make sure you are aware of all the costs, and in negotiations make sure you know who is paying for the shipping, and freight insurance etc. Also there is likely to be import duty when the goods arrive in the UK.

Trade organisations

In every industry there will be associations and organisations specific to the industry you are working in, and they are likely to be a key source of information for you with regard to sourcing products. Also look for trade magazines, there is one called The Trader, which will give you a great list of potential suppliers, more info can be found at www.thetrader.co.uk.

9 - MARKETING

Creating a marketing plan
Below we will cover the key online and offline marketing activities to get you started, however it is important for you to put a marketing plan in place so that you can track, measure and manage your marketing activities so that you get to know what works.

I advise that you create a monthly marketing plan that outlines the marketing activities you are going to do each month and the costs involved. At the end of each month note next to each activity the results you have got, this will help you measure which marketing is most effective for you.

It is important to always be doing some marketing activity as if you are doing nothing then your business is unlikely to grow and it is only a matter of time before your business starts to decline.

Marketing - ONLINE

Creating a website
A website is a must for any business today. Your website is where potential customers will go to check you out; in my eyes the website has replaced the traditional brochure. Also nowadays depending on your industry you can use your website to sell products or services and help you build the relationship with your customer.

You have two options:
1. Do it yourself
2. Get a web developer

For both options it is important to have a plan, as this will help you or your web developer to put your site together efficiently and effectively. Remember though even if you get a web developer to do it for you, you will still need to write the content to go into your website.

Your plan should include the following:
- What colours do you want to use?
- What layout do you want? – header, footer, 3 columns in between
- What pages do you want? As a minimum I would suggest:
    - Welcome/Home page – keep it simple, include a brief overview of what you do. It is important that this home page includes key words to help you get found when people search online for you
    - Products/Services – a list of the services and products you offer with the features and benefits
    - About – a bit about you, to provide credibility to your potential customers
    - Contact – a contact form and full contact details so that clients can get hold of you
- Do you want pictures? When using pictures on any online or offline marketing do make sure you have permission to use them, I have known businesses get fined £0000's for using images when they didn't have permission to use.

Remember to keep it simple for the first draft, you can amend at a later date; however do keep in mind your customer and what they want, as it has to appeal to them. Another question to answer is what do you want your website to do? For the professional service firm it's all about creating a brochure site, and capturing contact details so that you can keep in touch. However for many businesses nowadays the website is much more and potentially is used for e-commerce, and full lead generation and sales funnel.

A Practical Guide to Setting Up Your Business

What you need to create your website?
- Domain name – you can buy this from 123-reg, 1&1, or Go-Daddy
- Software to create your website – e.g. using Weebly, Wix and WordPress
- Hosting – this is provided free when you use the Weebly, Wix and WordPress software to create your website

For the DIY option there are 3 platforms that I recommend, they are Weebly, Wix and WordPress. My favourite being Weebly (www.weebly.com) as if you want to change the theme (the look/colours) after you have started you can, whereas on WIX once you have chosen your theme you appear to have to stick with it. WordPress seems to be the most popular option that small businesses use, however to get a lot of the features there are extra charges. Weebly has a pro version which gives you access to more features which I use and costs less than £100 a year.

On Weebly you create your website in WYSIWYG (What you see is what you get), i.e. if you want text you drag a text box from the side panel onto the main page and start typing, as simple as that! Weebly will give you a free domain that ends in weebly.com, however I would recommend that you pay for a domain, I personally use www.123-reg.co.uk for my domain names and email. The help in Weebly will give you the information to link your domain to your website, follow the instructions and you can't go wrong (hopefully)!

The do it yourself option gives you complete control of the content and you can change things easily when you want to, be careful though, you can end up spending hours playing around with different layouts, themes, and content, it is important to stick to your plan and get the basic information on and publish it, you can spend the time perfecting it in due course.

For the web developer option I advise that you get quotes from more than one developer as it is likely that the prices will vary significantly. If you can give them the plan of what you want it will make the process much more efficient and you are more likely to get the website that you want. Many developers now do offer business owners a CMS system which is a Content Management System, this means the developer will set the website up and get it working but they will show you how to amend the text content so that you can keep it up to date yourself. Normally when using a web developer you will have to pay initially for the set up (and training if a CMS), and then there is normally a monthly or annual hosting and maintenance fee. This seems to vary significantly from developer to developer. Costs for the web developer option can range anywhere from a few hundred pounds to thousands of pounds. Always read the small print outlining what they will do for the fee to make sure you are going to get what you think you have asked for.

Using Google analytics

Google analytics is a service offered by Google which generates a piece of HTML code that you can then put into your website which will track the visitors to your site with regard to where they visited your site from, e.g. which site they were referred from, or whether they typed the web address in directly. It will also tell you how many visitors you have had on your site and which pages they visited. This is a free service. If you have used a web developer it would be useful to ask them to set this up for you at the same time as they do the website but make sure you have access to the Google analytics

A Practical Guide to Setting Up Your Business

reports so that you can log in and have a look whenever you want to.

Google analytics uses 'cookies' to capture the information therefore you must ensure you have a cookie disclaimer when collecting peoples data. More information can be found here www.ico.org.uk/for-the-public/online/cookies/

Google Adwords for advertising
Google Adwords advertising is where you pay Google to place your advert at the top of a search results. You will notice that there are sometimes a few search results at the top of a page, and smaller adverts down the right hand side, these are the Adwords ads that someone has paid for them to be there.

You are in control of what you spend per day and you only pay when someone clicks on your advert. You can have various adverts running at once so you can then see what is working best for you. You can also have different campaigns running too so that you can track everything you do. It works on the basis of bids. I.e. the higher the amount you are willing to pay the more likely you are to be at the top. You can also set daily limits too. For example on one of my businesses I set my limit to £5 per day and at £1.50 per click as there are larger companies on there too in the same industry with the same key words that have a similar bid rate. If you are in a unique market without competition then you could end up only having to put a 50p per click amount in. When setting this up Google will advise you on the rate you will need to use for it to be effective.

Your adverts must have your key words in them. Key words being the words that someone will type in to the Google search box. Google will also give you lots of analysis on key words too. Setting up a Google account is free, so sign up and have a look, you've got nothing to lose. More information can be found at www.google.co.uk/adwords

Social Media
Firstly decide on which social media platforms you are going to start with, as there are now hundreds of social media sites and there are many now specialising in specific areas/niches. The key is to work out on what social media platforms your ideal client uses. You can research this online.

The main sites to consider first are:
- LinkedIn
- Twitter
- Facebook
- You Tube (video marketing is now becoming very popular)

I advise that you only use two to start with until you find your feet with your social media plan.

Remember social media is not about selling; it is about creating a community and building relationships. As with all marketing you need a plan of action to keep you focused and ensure you are using social media effectively in your business.

Your social media plan needs to highlight what you aim to achieve and how you are going to achieve it. For example one main aim may be to build a following on Twitter to whom you can provide value to with links to interesting articles. You can achieve this by following people that provide useful content that you can re-tweet, and look at who follow them and try to connect with them as they are potentially your target customer.

A Practical Guide to Setting Up Your Business

Most social media platforms are free to join, therefore choose the two you wish to try first and set up your free account.

You need to be consistent with your message and post regularly. Social media is not something that you can do once and then forget about, you have to be pro-active. There are tools out there now that help you automate your social media e.g. social oomph, Tweet Deck, and Hootsuite to name a few, that will allow you to post items at a future date, however you must ensure that the posts are relevant to your followers and post in a timely manner.

Marketing – OFFLINE

Business cards
Business cards, as with all printed material, need to be consistent with your brand. Once you have your logo you can create your business cards via an online site such as www.moo.com or www.vistaprint.co.uk. Whoever you use though I advise that you just order a small quantity at first e.g. 100 not 1000 as you don't really know whether you will like them, and also at this point you don't know many you will use. You can always re-order a larger quantity at a later date, I say this as I have in the past been unhappy with the cards even though I had proofed them, or afterwards realised I should have added further information on to them.

As a minimum you should include:
- Logo
- Name of business
- Your name
- Telephone
- Email address
- Website address

A Practical Guide to Setting Up Your Business

- Tag line (if you have one)
- Profession or an indication of what you do

The trend today seems to be to use both sides and why not use both sides to give further information even if it is a picture of what you do, as you need to get your card to stand out over others. I currently use www.moo.com and I use their small half size cards, not only are they cheaper almost everyone I give one to comments on it saying it is unusual, this means I will hopefully stay in their mind longer because of the unusual card. One thing I would say though is always use a high quality card weight of card, and a good finish such as a gloss finish as that card needs to show you have made an effort and feel good by the person that takes it off you. A cheap flimsy card is unlikely to make the right impression.
Remember you only get one chance to make a first impression.

Creating a brochure
Brochures can be useful when having face to face meetings with prospects however nowadays your website can virtually replace any paper brochures you may need therefore think wisely before going to print. Don't get me wrong a beautifully produced brochure can be a real asset to leave with a prospect if it contains useful information in an easy to read format, and may well include information which isn't as easily readable on your website. However printing costs can go in to the £100's and therefore for the start up business it may be something that you don't need straight away.

Networking
It is no word of a lie when I say the most valuable thing I did for generating new customers was networking. There are only a handful of clients that I can specifically link to a networking event I have attended, but by getting out there and talking about what you

A Practical Guide to Setting Up Your Business

are doing works. It's not necessarily the people in the room that become clients but they know people who know people, who know people and word gets round!

Start with finding networking events in your local area and book on them. There are many networks out there where you have to become a member, however most let you go to a couple of meetings first to see if you like it before having to join up. I suspect though you will find a good handful of local networking events that are just pay as you go, and don't require any annual memberships. It is also likely that when you go to your first networking event being a 'Newbie' people will offer many other local networking events to you.

Make sure you go prepared with your business cards, and prepare an elevator pitch so that when someone asks you what you do you have a 1 minute explanation of your business you can tell them. Many networking events give you the opportunity to do a 1 minute round where you stand up in front of everyone and give them your 1 minute elevator pitch.

Key points to a great elevator pitch:
- Tell them your name and company name and what you do
- Tell them how you help people, what pain do you take away
- Tell them why you are different to your competition – what your USP is
- Tell them who you are looking to do business with
- Give them a call to action – e.g. make reference to go to your website for more information

You could also video your elevator pitch for practice, and if you are happy with it put it on You Tube. You can then use the You Tube video on your website so your website can be working for you 24/7.

A Practical Guide to Setting Up Your Business

Here is a list of networks and network finding sites for you to have a look over:
- 4networking.biz - www.4networking.biz
- BNI - www.bni.co.uk
- Federation of Small business (although not a pure networking organisation they do offer networking in most regions) - www.fsb.org.uk/regions
- Chamber of Commerce - www.britishchambers.org.uk

The following website is very good at showing you relevant events in your area - www.findnetworkingevents.com

In Worcestershire specifically we have the following organisations that offer networking opportunities:
- Malvern Small Business Forum
- Malvern Women in Business
- Find It In Worcestershire
- Hereford and Worcester Chamber of Commerce

My advice is to go to one of everything. See what suits you but keep in mind, are the people there your ideal customer, or likely to be connected to your ideal customer? You can't do it all so choose the ones that you like best and try it for a period of time, then review it near the end of your first year and ask did it give me the results I was looking for? If not, then for your second year move on and try something different. It is no good spending time and money on networking if you do not get a benefit, whether that benefit is new clients or just general support, it can be very lonely setting up a business and networking sometimes becomes a good support network and keeps you motivated even if it doesn't generate any actual leads.

A Practical Guide to Setting Up Your Business

Networking isn't all about getting new business, sometimes it is about support and enjoying the company of other business owners just to stay motivated and help build relationships.

Remember people buy from people they know, like and trust and therefore you must remember to build relationships over time and nurture those relationships with key introducers (introducers being people that are likely to refer business to you).

Networking is NOT a quick fix, but works on so many levels.

Remember to follow up with people you connect with a few days after meeting them at a networking event. I like to connect with people via LinkedIn, so that I then know how I can connect with them if I need to in future if I don't have their business card to hand. You could also ask if they are happy to go on your mailing list and add them accordingly, this is another tool to help build your relationship with them.

Marketing Summary
Getting your first customers could be one of the hardest things you do, and so as a minimum I recommend the following 3 step plan:
1. Get website live
2. Get business cards printed
3. Network, Network, Network!

And remember you will need to do a number of marketing initiatives at the same time to give you a better chance of success.

10 - SALES

Your marketing activity helps you build relationships with potential customers and tells people about what you do. It should generate you leads and then it is then your sales process or sales funnel that will turn them into paying customers.

So your marketing has generated the leads, you should then follow this up with a telephone call to organise a meeting for you to discuss your services further, or maybe you have got their permission for you to put them on to your email list, and you then use a series of emails to get clients to buy your products or sign up for your services.

If a client says 'No' it often doesn't mean no forever it just means no at the moment, this is where an effective CRM system (which I talk about in the next section) can help you track your leads so that you can follow up accordingly and in a timely fashion.

Some tools that are useful when trying to turn a lead into a paying customer are:
- ✓ Sales scripts
- ✓ Price lists
- ✓ Sales funnels

A sales script is useful more so when you have a team of staff and you need to make sure you are all being consistent in your approach to sales. The sales script will outline a list of potential questions that you can ask and also help to build rapport with the client. Try to make them open questions, i.e. questions that require more than a yes or no answer. The first set of questions should ask the potential customer about their situation and what they are looking for; it will also be a fact find to get basic contact information

A Practical Guide to Setting Up Your Business

Examples are:
- Ask for contact details (if you don't already have them) e.g. name, business name, address, email address, telephone number
- What type of business are you in?
- How long have you been in business?
- What type of business do you specialise in?
- What help do you need in your business?
- What service are you looking for?
- What products are you looking for?

You can then tell them about the services you can offer them and how you can help them, you can also tell them about the payment terms and any other important information that you need to. The second sets of questions are all about the close, to get the potential customer to say yes and sign up with you.

Examples are:
- What do you think about what we can offer you?
- Which product/service do you think is best for you?
- Is this something you are looking for?
- How soon are you looking to go ahead with the service/product?
- Would you like to go ahead if you can pay over 3 months?
- Have you got any questions about anything we have covered so far?

Once you have got them to say yes it is important to tell them what will happen next, i.e. they will receive a proposal letter from you outlining what you will do for them, or the product will be with them within 7 days etc. This part is all about managing customer

A Practical Guide to Setting Up Your Business

expectations and making sure you then exceed them with excellent customer service.

If you are selling digital products and use a CRM system like Agile CRM or Infusionsoft you should be able to do your entire sales funnel via emails and the software will automate almost the whole process.

Summary:
- ✓ Start with open questions to find out what the customer's needs are
- ✓ Review the answers and tell them about how you can help them
- ✓ Next ask questions to try and close the sale
- ✓ Once you have a 'yes' advise the customer what happens next

11 - COMMUNICATIONS & TECHNOLOGY

Email
Email is now an integral part of business communications. I always advise that you get an email address that matches your domain. It does cost money but looks so much more professional than using a Gmail, or Hotmail email address. You normally get your email address from the same company you bought your domain name from.

As emails are now part of day to day communications and have in many cases replaced the traditional letter, you must make sure that your business information is put on the email. I suggest you create an email signature that automatically comes up when you start a new email so that all the information is on there automatically.

You need to include, your name if you are a sole trader, or the names of the partners if you are a partnership, the company name if a limited company along with your company registration number. Also your VAT number if applicable and your registered office and business trading address. It is also good to include your contact details such as telephone number and a link to your website or web address.

Business stationery
In my business I have never had professional letterheads printed as most of my correspondence is via email. Compliments slips are useful. If you have your logo you can create your own letterhead and compliments slips in word, however make sure you buy some good quality paper e.g. greater than 100gsm in weight as even though you're going to print it yourself you want it to be of good quality, also I would suggest you invest in a laser printer as this will

A Practical Guide to Setting Up Your Business

give you a better quality of print. In my experience Brother laser printers seem to be the best value for money and running costs, and if you can afford to buy a duplex version (one that prints on both sides) then you will find it is worthwhile.

If however you find in the first few months you are using a lot of letterheads then it may be worth while getting some professionally printed, however to start with don't feel that you have to have it because you ought to, always ask yourself is it a necessity before going ahead with something.

Telephone
There are many options available to you with regard to telecommunications, the one thing I will say though is that it is not wise to use your home phone number or personal mobile number otherwise you will never be able to take a break from your business.

The most cost effective way I have found is to have a remote landline number that automatically comes through to a pay as you go mobile. This way you can get a number with your area code, which is very useful if you want people to know your business is local, however any calls that come through to your new pay as you go mobile you know to answer with your business name so that you always appear professional, you can also put an answer phone message on that phone specific to your business. There are fees per incoming call but they are minimal in the scale of things, and if you have a personal mobile on contract with unlimited minutes you can always say you will call them back. If you use 141 at the beginning of the number you dial the person you are calling does not get to see your personal mobile number.

I currently use DBS Chess Telecom (www.dbs-uk.co.uk/telecoms/local-ghost-virtual-numbers.html), and I can't

A Practical Guide to Setting Up Your Business

fault the service, note though there are additional fees for low call volumes and fees for cancellation. There are many other providers out there, just make sure you read the terms and conditions before signing up to ensure you are not tying yourself in to a long term contract.

Using a remote landline service seems to be cheaper than getting a second landline installed, and it means you can take your calls wherever you are. The estimated cost is £15 set up fee then £10 per month.

Computers
For almost all businesses you are going to need a computer or laptop to be able to run your business effectively and efficiently.

I always advise that you have a separate computer just for business use so that there can be no accidental mishaps e.g. deleting data, emailing files accidentally etc. if other members of your family use the same computer.

Dropbox is a fantastic piece of software that allows you to share files with other people, it can act like a mini server so if you intend to take on staff, and you can share your files with other people and you can access all your files wherever you are. Please be aware though of data protection advice with regard to where confidential data is stored in the world and check that if you use Dropbox you will still comply with data protection regulations.

On that point, as it has come up in many conversations with regard to where my data was being held, I bought a WD My Cloud NAS Drive, which acts as a mini server in my office and so all client information is held on this WD drive in my office, so I know exactly where it is being stored.

It is also important to ensure that you have a backup; I believe with Dropbox Pro, you can access previous versions of your documents for up to 30 days, however for many businesses it may be worth having a proper backup elsewhere. I use Livedrive, who do a back up of my WD My Cloud NAS drive, and they state that they comply with the UK data protection regulation which suggests the data is held in the UK.

You also need to ensure you have virus protection such as Norton, to help keep your data safe. There are free versions if you can't afford a premium version however you do need to make sure you have something.

Also make sure you use secure passwords for the various things you will be signing up for. Make sure you use a mixture of capital letters, small letter, symbols and numbers, don't use your pets name!

CRM Systems

If you are going to be a continually growing business with more than a hand full of customers then you are likely to need a CRM (customer relationship management) system.

A CRM system will help you track your leads through to becoming a customer, and then help you build and maintain the relationship with your customers.

There are various options available to you. You could simply use an excel spreadsheet or simple Microsoft Access database, however there are much more sophisticated products available now online that you can programme to send out emails automatically to guide customers through your sales funnel. Of course it depends on what you are doing for your business as to how good a system is needed, however my advice is to think long term as if you put the right system in now that will do what you need it to do now and when you grow will be ready for growth, rather than having to change systems in the future, so get it right from day one.

I bet you are saying that is easier said than done? Well write a checklist of things you will potentially use your CRM system for example:
- Signing people up to your mailing list
- Emailing them special offers
- Sending them emails/letters asking them to send you information
- Getting them to sign up for a service
- Review emails that have been sent

Then you can find a system that will do what you need. There are two online systems that come highly recommended, they are InfusionSoft and Agile CRM these are especially good if you are an online business as they both help you with your sales process. I have also used Solve 360 from Norada which links into Google mail and indexes your emails into the CRM system so that you and your team can see all the emails from each of the clients.

Some CRM systems also allow you to create templates for letters and emails that you will use a lot, so if it has this feature it would save you a lot of time.

Mailchimp
If you do not require a full CRM system then you are still likely to need an email platform so that you can send out bulk emails, or campaigns. I recommend Mailchimp as there is a free version you can use which will suffice for most new businesses. It allows you to create lovely emails to send to clients for monthly newsletters, or to

tell them about new products etc. It will also allow you to track how many people open the emails, so you can see which emails work for you and which don't. Using a service like this will also help stop your email address being blacklisted, as if you send lots of bulk emails direct from your email provider it can potentially mark you as a spammer and your emails will end up going into their junk folder. You must remember though that you must get the person's permission before you put them on your email list and start emailing them.

More information can be found at – www.mailchimp.com

Also with Mailchimp you can create a piece of code from the Mailchimp website that you can put on your website to help you collect email addresses, this means when a potential customer signs up to your email list their email address is put straight into the corresponding email list.

Skype
Skype allows you to make video and audio calls. It is something that I use almost daily in my business as it allows me to communicate with clients effectively and at minimal cost. It does need a good internet connection and you need a good microphone. It allows you to share screens, so if you are training someone on how to use a piece of software they can share their screen with you so that they can be in the driving seat and you can then talk them thorough how to use it. It really is a useful tool and means location isn't so much a barrier to doing business as you can still keep a personal touch using a webcam to stay in touch, and allow you to work more effectively and reduce your travel costs.

12 - EQUIPMENT

We have already spoken about needing a computer or laptop; however there is a list of other equipment pieces you need to consider:

Computer equipment
- Additional computers for staff
- Printers
- Scanners
- Label printers (if despatching products)
- Webcam for Skype meetings

Sales equipment
- Cash register
- Card machine (consider paypal as they now do terminals that are cost effective)
- Barcode scanner

Office furniture
- Desks
- Bookcase
- Filing cabinets
- Boardroom table and chairs
- Kitchen supplies – e.g. kettle, mugs, coffee machine
- Reception chairs and coffee table

Fixtures (e.g. for trade counters)
- Display cabinets
- Racking
- Storage containers

13 - PREMISES

You will need to consider whether you need premises, just storage or an office. Ask yourself could you work from home initially while you are getting started. I worked from home for the first 15 months, however after taking on a part time member of staff I found it wasn't ideal for us both to be working at our dining room tables, so I went on the waiting list and when one came up I took a small office in a serviced office building. We have two desks, two chairs and a bookcase and its costs us around £300 per month, and it has been 100% worth the money, as more people have got to know who we are and so have got more business from being based there, so you could say it has paid for itself.

When looking at premises you need to consider the following:
- How much space do you need?
- How big do you expect to grow and will it be big enough for you?
- What are the lease terms?

Be very aware of the lease terms and find out about break clauses as if things do not go to plan you could be left with years left on a lease that you are personally liable for. When taking on a lease for premises I would always recommend you seek legal advice to go over the contract before signing.

Another consideration when taking on premises is Business Rates. Some councils offer small businesses something called 'small business rates relief', which means you do not need to pay business rates if you are a small business, however I believe not all councils offer this, so please check with your local council, as this is another cost and can be significant.

A Practical Guide to Setting Up Your Business

Also consider the cost of telephone lines, or mobile reception if using the remote landline I talked about earlier in the book, broadband, electricity costs etc. If you are in a serviced office the only additional expense you are likely to have is extra for a telephone line, however if you are taking on premises in their entirety who will need to also pay for all the utilities too, so a £500 per month office to rent could realistically work out to be £700 once you have added all the other expenses on, plus you will have the outlay of the furniture too, therefore if you can make a serviced office work for you, it is likely to be the most effective option for you to start with.

If you decide you do not need premises, consider where you are going to hold meetings with clients, will you use a local cafe, or are you happy to invite them into your home. Before I got the office I found a lot of the time I could go to the client's premises, or I had various options, such as a local cafe, there is also a pub near a major motorway junction that is full of business people meeting people for a coffee or breakfast and doing business, and also look for serviced offices that have a pay as you go service for you to use their boardroom if you need something a bit more professional.

14 - PRICING

One thing we haven't discussed yet that links significantly to sales is pricing, as I felt this was more appropriate to cover this in the numbers section here.

Pricing
Setting your price can be a tricky thing to master; the way you work it out is going to be slightly different if you are a service based organisation to a product based organisation, however as a starting point both involve calculating your breakeven point, which I will go through with you shortly. The breakeven point is a level (in hours or units) where total income equals total expenses. Once you have reached the number of hours or units you will then be making a profit, if you do not sell enough to reach your breakeven point you will be trading at a loss, so it is a really useful calculation to do to give you an idea of the amount of work you will need to do to become profitable.

Service based business
For a service based business the first thing to consider is how many hours you want to work and what income do you want to achieve? We can then put this into a breakeven formula to see what this would look like for your business. Once you have done your breakeven analysis (I will show you this shortly) and decided your potential price, you need to try and find out what your nearest competitors are charging so that you can make sure you aren't out pricing yourself out of the market, or if you are your marketing materials will need to make it extremely clear the extra or additional service or quality they will get to justify your price.

A Practical Guide to Setting Up Your Business

Product based business

For a product based business you need to work out what your costs of buying the product will be so that you can work out what the breakeven point is, and then as with a service based business find out what your competitors are charging. I'm not saying you should match your competitors price however if there is a recommended retail price (RRP) then that is a good starting point for testing the market, you can always move your price down or up.

With both service and product based businesses remember your USP, as your USP can mean you can charge higher prices than your competitors.

To be able to work out your breakeven point you need to compile a list of the following costs using the template below:

Definitions:

Variable costs / direct costs are the costs per unit to buy a product or in a service based business the hourly rate that you want to earn or have to pay sub-contractors. Direct costs go up or down in line with sales.

Fixed costs / overheads are costs that you will have to pay whether you sell anything or not, i.e. they are costs that stay the same no matter how many products. There are a few exceptions for example your travel costs and marketing costs are likely to be higher the more sales you make, however overheads aren't normally directly related to making a sale

List of costs for a service based business:

Variable costs per hour

A Practical Guide to Setting Up Your Business

- The potential hourly rate you want to earn or hourly rate for a subcontractor – e.g. £20 per hour

Total variable costs = £20 per unit
Sales price aim = £30 per hour

Fixed costs/overheads per year
- Staff wages
- Rent, rates, heat & light
- General travelling & subsistence
- Stationery, printing, postage
- Professional fees, legal, accountancy
- Repairs and maintenance
- Bank charges and finance costs
- Sundry

For illustrative purposes let's estimate overheads being a total of £10,000 per year

List of costs for a product based business:

Variable costs per unit
- Purchases/stock/materials - £7 per unit
- Packaging - £1 per unit
- Carriage/haulage - £2 per unit

Total variable costs = £10 per unit

Sales price RRP = £20 per unit

Fixed costs/overheads per year
- Directors/owners salary/drawings
- Rent, rates, heat & light

A Practical Guide to Setting Up Your Business

- Motor expenses
- Travelling & subsistence
- Stationery, printing, postage
- Professional fees, legal, accountancy
- Repairs and maintenance
- Bank charges and finance costs
- Sundry

For illustrative purposes let's estimate overheads being a total of £10,000 per year

Once you have completed the above list of costs you can now put the figures in to the breakeven equation.

The Breakeven equation is:

Fixed Costs / (Sales Price - Variable Cost) = Breakeven point in units/hours

So we know what the fixed costs are, and we know what the variable costs are so we can play with the sales price to see what the breakeven point will be

Here is an example for a service based business:

Fixed Costs £10,000 / (Sales Price £30 – Variable Cost £20) = Breakeven point in hours = 1000 hours

This means 1000 hours / 52 weeks per year = 19 hours per week just to breakeven

If you are happy to be working in your business full time, working 19 hours a week to breakeven seems reasonable, and this is after

A Practical Guide to Setting Up Your Business

paying yourself £20 per hour too. If you worked 29 hours a week the extra 10 hours over breakeven point will all be profit as all your overheads have already been covered by the 19 hours you have already worked, so the 10 hours per week x (Sales price £30 – Variable Costs £20) = £100 per week, which would give you an estimated profit of £5,200 for the year.

If after looking at what your competitors are charging you feel £30 per hour is too expensive, and actually £25 would be a more reasonable price to charge, let's see how that calculation would look as that £5 difference in price has a significant effect on the amount of work you will need to do.

Fixed Costs £10,000 / (Sales Price £25 – Variable Cost £20) = Breakeven point in hours = 2000 hours

This means 2000 hours / 52 weeks = 38 hours per week just to breakeven

So as you can see just a £5 reduction in sales price means you will have to work twice as hard just to reach breakeven, therefore at £25 per hour as a sales price you would have to be happy with just earning £20 per hour and have no extra profit afterwards.

Here is an example for a product based business:

Fixed Costs £10,000 / (Sales Price £20 – Variable Cost £10) = Breakeven point in units = 1000 units

This means you would need to sell 19 units per week to cover your overheads

A Practical Guide to Setting Up Your Business

Let's now see what would happen if you were only able to charge £15 per unit

Fixed Costs £10,000 / (Sales Price £15 – Variable Cost £10) = Breakeven point in units = 2000 units

This means you would need to sell 38 units per week to breakeven. So again you would need to work twice as hard just to cover your overheads.

Summary of breakeven analysis
From this analysis you can see that you can use the above formula to try different sales prices to see what your targets will need to be to breakeven. For a product based business I would suggest that you also include what you want to take out of the business as salary/drawings in the overheads (as listed), where as for the service based business we are including the hourly rate you want to earn in with the variable costs.

Other pricing considerations
As previously mentioned you need to keep in mind what your USP is. Because of your USP are you able to charge a higher price? In a service based business you will often hear a phrase value added pricing, this is where you don't charge an hourly rate but charge a price that reflects the value the client receives. This really is a science in its own right, my suggestion is with any pricing you need to start with your breakeven point, then research your market and see what your service is worth on the open market place, and then add a bit more on to the sales price. You can always bring your price down when you negotiate with clients (as long as it isn't lower than what is needed to breakeven) however it is harder to put your price up.

A Practical Guide to Setting Up Your Business

In a service based business you should always try to increase your prices slightly year on year to cover inflation, and in a product based business you will need to review your prices every time to have a price increase from your supplier.

For a product based business you can also use a 'Mark Up' on the cost price to work out a sales price, for example if your product cost £10 and you put a 50% mark up on it, this would make the sales price £15 per unit, however you will still need to put these figures into your breakeven analysis to see how many units you would need to sell at £15 per unit to breakeven.

For businesses that are selling multiple products, I would suggest that you split your overheads between the products, i.e. if you are selling 10 different products and your overheads are £10,000 you would allocate £1000 of overheads against each product.

15 - ACCOUNTING

Record keeping

It is important from day one that you keep accurate financial records. By keeping your financial information up to date it will help make sure you:
- record all of your expenses and income so that you pay the right amount of tax
- help you see quickly what you are owed by others and how much you owe them

Also if you need to ask the bank for a bank loan or credit they will want to see your financial information too and ultimately by keeping good records it should save your accountant time and therefore you should have lower accountancy costs.

You may ask why you need to keep records. The answer – well as a sole trader you have to fill in a tax return and the law says that you should keep all the records and documents you need to enter the right figures on to your return and if HMRC need to check your return, they can ask to see the records you used to complete it. As a director of a company you have a statutory duty to keep accurate company records.

There also are now penalties if you do not keep adequate records, and penalties for any inaccuracies on your tax return, however people do make mistakes and HMRC say that you will not have to pay a penalty if you can show them that you took reasonable care to get your return right. The main ways in which you can show you've taken reasonable care include, keeping full and accurate records which are regularly updated and saved securely, and showing proof you have asked an accountant or adviser if there is something you are not sure of.

A Practical Guide to Setting Up Your Business

The law does not say how you must keep your records, but the guidance does say that most records can now be kept electronically e.g. on a computer or any storage device such as a memory stick as long as it captures all the information on the document (front and back), and allows the information to be presented to HMRC in a readable format, if they need to see it. I would always advise that you have a backup copy of all records too just in case.

As a general rule, you should keep your records for a minimum of six years.

The types of records you need to keep depend on the size and complexity of your business and the different taxes that you have to pay, however here are some examples that are relevant to most businesses:

A record of all sales and takings, including cash receipts for example:
- till rolls
- sales invoices
- bank statements
- paying-in slips

A record of all purchases and expenses, including cash purchases for example:
- receipts and purchase invoices
- bank and credit card statements
- chequebook stubs
- mileage records

HMRC sets out guidance with regard to basic record keeping. Here is a link to the HMRC guidance - https://www.gov.uk/government/uploads/system/uploads/attachment_data/file/366523/record-keeping.pdf

A Practical Guide to Setting Up Your Business

How to keep records

With regard to actually keeping your records you have five options:
1. Keep manual hand written records on paper
2. Use spreadsheets
3. Use a computerised accounting system such Sage, Quickbooks or VT Software
4. Use an online accounting system such as XERO, Freeagent, Kashflow or Quickbooks Online
5. Outsource it to a bookkeeper or accountant

If you are going to be VAT registered then I would always advise that you use option 3, 4 or 5. The reason for this is because sometimes you will get late items that need to go on the next VAT return and it isn't always easy to keep track of these adjustments if you are preparing VAT returns with hand written records or spreadsheets. The software will track these late items for you and add them to the next VAT return for you.

1. If you are keeping **manual records** I would advise that you buy a cash book (here is a link to one on Amazon as an example - http://www.amazon.co.uk/Rhino-keeping-accounts-treble-reverse/dp/B004NDV0N6/ref=sr_1_10?ie=UTF8&qid=1460221116&sr=8-10&keywords=cash+book) and on one half/side of the book record sales information and the other half/side record purchase information, for both sides I would have headings that include the following:
- Date
- Name of customer or supplier
- Description of item sold or bought
- Amount
- Running total

© 2016 The Business Pod Limited

A Practical Guide to Setting Up Your Business

By keeping a running total on each page you can carry this forward on to the next page to keep a running total for the year, so in theory you can take your total income, less total expenses to give you an idea of what profit you have made. NOTE though this will not give you an accurate profit figure as some items that you buy may be capital in nature and therefore not allowable, and also there will be other year end adjustments that your accountant will include such as use of home, accountancy fee accrual, depreciation on fixed assets, stock movements etc. but it should give you a ball park idea of your profitability.

If you are VAT registered and want to use manual records instead of just one column for an amount you will need three for Gross Amount, VAT Amount and Net Amount. You will also need to make sure that without fail you have a proper VAT invoice for items that you are going to be claiming VAT back on. Also if calculating VAT I would keep a running total for each quarter and start a new page and new running total for the next VAT return.

When using manual records you will need to create a sales invoice to customers on your computer using Word, or by using a Duplicate invoice book. I suggest you keep copies of your receipts/purchase invoices in a folder in date order or in an envelope for each month so that if you need to refer to it in the future it should be easy to find.

If you are going to be VAT registered I would advise that you speak to an accountant for further advice as there are various schemes that you can use depending on your type and size of business.

2. If you wish to use **spreadsheets** I suggest you find a template online, unless you are competent in creating formulas in excel in which case you can create your own. I would advise that you set up

A Practical Guide to Setting Up Your Business

two spreadsheets one to record income and one to record purchases in a very similar manner as outlined for manual records above.

3. If you wish to use a **computerised accounting system** such as sage, please ensure you receive at least basic training on the software which should include the following:
- How to create, update, post and send sales invoices
- How to put on purchase invoices
- Which codes to use for different VAT rates
- How to post bank transactions
- How to reconcile bank
- How to put a journal on for monthly wages
- How to enter items that are paid for by owners/directors

Failure to get training before you use the software and not having accountancy knowledge normally means things get posted incorrectly and therefore the reports you can run will not give you accurate information. It is really easy to post things to the wrong place if you don't understand the different ledgers (modules on sage), and how they link to the profit and loss and balance sheet, this means that when you give a backup of it to your accountant at the year end they will have to make many adjustments which will be time consuming to put your figures right, so much so I have actually started jobs from scratch on occasions because the bank didn't reconcile, journals weren't posted and so to ensure the accounts were correct I prepared them from scratch.

4. If you wish to use an **online accounting system** most will offer you an automatic bank feed, this means your bank activity will come into the software automatically, this will save you time, and make it easy to do bank reconciliation. XERO by far makes it the easiest to

A Practical Guide to Setting Up Your Business

do a bank reconciliation; Freeagent, Kashflow and Freeagent are all more similar to the way you would do it on sage.

Again if using an online system please get basic training before using. XERO offers a fantastic You Tube Channel with training videos and has many online webinar and training options. XERO is my preferred option for an online accounting system as it is by far the easiest and most user friendly for non-accountants to use.

5. If you are not confident dealing with financial paperwork or just don't really want to do your bookkeeping then you can always **outsource it to a bookkeeper or your accountant**. Most will charge you an hourly rate; however some accountants will now offer you a fixed monthly fee for bookkeeping in with your fee for your year end accounts and tax return.

Preparing accounts
Management accounts are accounts that a business prepares throughout the year monthly or quarterly so that you can keep an eye on the business' profitability. The larger the business the more important it is to prepare monthly management accounts. Preparing monthly or quarterly accounts also means that you can plan for any tax liabilities so that you are not left with a potentially unexpected tax bill.

Year end accounts are accounts that are prepared on an annual basis and the information is used to calculate any tax payable.

When preparing management accounts or your year end accounts there are two main financial statements that are prepared as standard, these are:
1. Profit and Loss Account (also now known as an Income Statement) - a profit and loss account contains details of all

of your income/sales into the business, less all of your allowable expenses
2. Balance Sheet - a balance sheet is a list of the assets and liabilities of the business, along with the equity and reserves.

Before we go any further here is some basic accounting terminology:

General:
- Customers – people that buy things from you
- Suppliers – businesses that you buy things from
- Trade debtors – customers that owe you money
- Trade Creditors – suppliers that you owe money to

Profit and loss items:
- Income – sales, turnover
- Cost of sales – direct costs, variable costs, purchases, sub-contractors
- Administrative expenses – overheads, rent, rates, utilities, stationery, computer costs, wages, legal fees, accountancy fees etc.
- Taxation – corporation tax for limited companies

Balance Sheet Items:
- Fixed assets – equipment, fixtures and fittings, motor vehicles
- Current assets – stock, cash at bank, trade debtors
- Current liabilities – bank overdraft, short term bank loans, trade creditors, hire purchase, corporation tax, PAYE due, VAT due
- Long term liabilities – loan term loans such as mortgages, for long term hire purchase

A Practical Guide to Setting Up Your Business

- Reserves - profits that are left after tax that could be paid to owners
- Equity – shares issued in a limited company

Here is an example of both financial statements. (Items in brackets on a profit and loss account e.g. (£0) mean they are expenses that reduce your profit) (Items in brackets on the balance sheet are either liabilities or drawings/dividends and they are items that are reducing the reserves/value of the business)

Profit & Loss Account:

A Practical Guide to Setting Up Your Business

Example Company Limited
Profit and Loss Account
for the year ended 31 December 2015

		2015 £
Turnover / Income / Sales		150,000
Cost of sales (variable / direct Costs)		
Purchases / Materials	(43,000)	
Increase in stocks	(5,000)	
Subcontractor costs	(1,000)	
Direct labour	(1,000)	(50,000)
Gross profit		100,000
Administrative expenses		
Employee costs:		
Wages and salaries	(15,000)	
Directors' salaries	(10,000)	
Pensions	(1,000)	
Bonuses	(1,000)	
Employer's NI	-	
Staff training and welfare	(1,000)	
Travel and subsistence	(1,000)	
Motor expenses	(1,000)	
Entertaining	(100)	
Premises costs:		
Rent	(12,000)	
Rates	(2,000)	
Light and heat	(1,000)	
Cleaning	(600)	
Use of home	(208)	

A Practical Guide to Setting Up Your Business

General administrative expenses:		
Telephone and fax	(500)	
Postage	(100)	
Stationery and printing	(400)	
Information and publications	(100)	
Subscriptions	(500)	
Bank charges	(80)	
Insurance	(450)	
Equipment expensed	(150)	
Equipment hire	(200)	
Software	(500)	
Repairs and maintenance	(250)	
Depreciation	(100)	
Bad debts	(100)	
Sundry expenses	(100)	
Legal and professional costs:		
Accountancy fees	(750)	
Solicitors fees	(200)	
Consultancy fees	(600)	
Advertising and PR	(2,000)	
Other legal and professional	(500)	(53,488)
Operating profit		46,512
Interest receivable		100
Interest payable		(250)
Profit on ordinary activities before taxation		46,362
Tax on profit on ordinary activities		(9,142)
Profit for the financial year		37,220

Balance Sheet:

A Practical Guide to Setting Up Your Business

Example Company Limited
Balance Sheet
as at 31 December 2015

	Notes	2015
		£
Fixed assets		
Tangible assets - Equipment		750
Current assets		
Stocks	5,000	
Debtors	2,000	
Cash at bank and in hand	1,450	
	8,450	
Creditors: amounts falling due within one year	(1,880)	
Net current assets		6,570
Net assets		7,320
Capital and reserves		
Called up share capital		100
Profit and loss account		37,220
Dividends/Drawings		(30,000)
Shareholders' funds		7,320

A Practical Guide to Setting Up Your Business

Allowable expenses

I get asked a lot 'Can you advise me on what expenses I can claim for?', and my answer is as follows, if you can 100% hand on heart say this expense is 100% purely for business purposes then it is normally allowable, there are of course exceptions to which I say, if you're not sure, put it in with your records, mark it with a '?' and then let your accountant advise you on this at your year end, or ask your accountant throughout the year.

If you have a current contract for your mobile phone in your personal name and you use it for business, you can work out how much you use it for business and put a pro-rata amount though as a business expense. You do need to substantiate this though, so if you say put 75% of the cost of your phone through the business and you ever have an HMRC investigation you would need to provide an itemised bill and be able to show that 75% of your calls are actually for business purposes, therefore always under estimate than over estimate.

The profit and loss account above lists the main categories of items that are allowable. Here is a link to HMRC which will give you further information - www.gov.uk/expenses-if-youre-self-employed/overview

If you are a limited company you do not want to put motor costs through the company unless it is for a van/commercial vehicle. You will need to keep a mileage log and claim mileage at 45p per mile up to 10,000 miles and 25p over 10,000 miles. As a sole trader your accountant may give you the option to put your vehicle in to your accounts if you are using the vehicle primarily for business use, this means you will be able to put all of your motor expenses through, but at the year end they will then add back am element of personal use, you must not do this if you are a limited company as it will

A Practical Guide to Setting Up Your Business

create a benefit in kind and the company and you personally will have additional tax to pay. With regard to vehicle expenses I advise that you speak to your accountant for the best advice for your specific circumstances.

If you work from home you can put through £4 per week through to contribute towards the cost of running your business from home. This is the maximum amount you can put through without HMRC potentially challenging the amount. You can put more through based on a calculation of costs such as light and heat, council tax, insurance, mortgage interest which is then pro-rata'd based on the number of rooms that are used for business purposes only, however please seek professional advice if wishing to use this method. Here is a link to some examples from HMRC's website - www.hmrc.gov.uk/manuals/bimmanual/bim47825.htm

Cash flow management
Cash flow is king, you can have a profit but be struggling for cash and so from day one you need to manage this.

When you are thinking of buying anything in your business my advice is to always ask yourself these two questions:
1. Do you NEED it, not do you want it, but do you actually NEED it?
2. Is it 100% necessary for the good of the business,

You don't need to have a coat stand in your office just because you think you ought to, it is not a necessity and you don't really need it, where as business cards are likely to be a necessity as you need something to give to people with your contact details on when you meet them.

Here are my tips for good cash flow management:

A Practical Guide to Setting Up Your Business

- ✓ Invoice customers as soon as you can once a job is completed.
- ✓ Depending on what you do, could you ask clients to pay 50% up front?
- ✓ Consider offering a small discount say 1% for early payment – this is one I wouldn't really advise you to do unless it is standard practice in your industry.
- ✓ Make sure your clients know your payment terms from day one and chase them if they are late paying. If you are using XERO for your bookkeeping there is a great XERO Add-On called Debtor Daddy that will automatically send out reminders to late paying clients.
- ✓ If you are paid by cheque make sure you pay it in as soon as you can as many cheques take up to 7 days to clear nowadays.
- ✓ When paying suppliers
- ✓ If you are holding a lot of old stock/products consider a sale or discounting to turn that stock back into cash so that you can buy new stock that will sell at a higher price.
- ✓ If you are in a very high growth business you may wish to consider Invoice Discounting or Factoring, this is where a company loans you X% of an invoice value before the customer pays you, and charges you for the privilege, it can be a useful thing to consider if you have very slow paying customers.

When starting up a new business you will have some set up costs, if you follow my advice in this book so far hopefully you will have got lots of tips on things that you can do yourself or resources that will help keep costs down for you, however there will be some costs which you need to make sure you have the funds available for.

A Practical Guide to Setting Up Your Business

Not only will you need some funds for set-up costs you will need some funds for 'Working Capital', working capital is the money that will allow your business to continue to trade while you are waiting for customers to pay you. In the ideal world it would be great if you can get terms with your suppliers that are longer than the terms you give to your customers so that you hopefully will have the money from your customer before you need to pay your supplier.

An example if you give your clients payment terms of 7 days, then try to get terms of 14 days or even 30 days with your suppliers, this is easier said than done especially being a new business, as many suppliers will not give new businesses trading terms and actually want you to pay on delivery or up front as they will see you as high risk to start with.

16 - FUNDING

There are many options for funding. Here is a summary of some of the options:

- Debt Finance – for example bank overdrafts, loans, this is probably the one most people think of, in my experience banks are still asking for personal guarantees on loans so just be aware of this.
- Equity finance – this is where you give a % of your ownership of the company in exchange for money in.
- Grants from government or non-profit organisations. These tend to be industry specific and for very specific purposes. There is normally a lot of paperwork to complete to apply for the grant.
- Friends and family – if you do go down this route make sure you are clear about the repayment terms so that there is no fall out in the future
- Asset finance – for example hire purchase where a loan is secured on the items of equipment or vehicles
- Crowd Funding is where you put your business proposal forward to a crowd funding portal and potentially a large number of individuals will all put in small amounts of money to fund your business. Interest is normally payable and repayment at a certain point in time.
- Peer to Peer Lending is a type of debt financing where you borrow money from an individual without the use of an official intermediary such as a bank. Peer to Peer lending works very similar to a normal bank loan.

HMRC provides a significant list of many funding sources that may be available to you on the following link - www.gov.uk/business-finance-support-finder

A Practical Guide to Setting Up Your Business

17 - FURTHER ADVICE AND SUPPORT

Further advice
Here is a list of organisations that can potentially help you further on your quest for business success:
- The Business Pod Limited – www.business-pod.co.uk
- British Chambers of Commerce - www.britishchambers.org.uk
- Federation of Small Businesses - www.fsb.org.uk
- British Insurance Brokers Association - www.biba.org.uk/find-insurance
- Companies House - www.gov.uk/topic/company-registration-filing/starting-company
- HM Revenue & Customs – www.hmrc.gov.uk
- Health and Safety Executive - www.hse.gov.uk
- Santander Bank - www.santander.co.uk
- HSBC Bank - www.hsbc.co.uk
- Beacon Accountancy & Tax – www.malvern-accountant.co.uk

Support
When you are starting a business on your own it is important to create a support network around you, whether that be by attending networking events, getting a mentor or getting support from others in your industry e.g. by joining a trade association.

You will have times when you find it difficult to stay motivated, so creating a good support network around you from day one is really important, so when you are having a bad day or week you will have someone you can talk to about it.

A Practical Guide to Setting Up Your Business

18 - SUMMARY FOR SUCCESS

We have covered a lot in this 20,000 word book and therefore I encourage you to seek professional advice when setting up your business from an accountant, or business adviser, as every individual has a different set of circumstances and an accountant can advise you on the best business structure for your individual needs. I can't stress the importance enough of getting your structure right from day one as if you don't you can end up with large tax liabilities or be in a situation financially you didn't expect to be in. Also by getting an accountant on board from day one it means you have someone you can talk to throughout your business journey and they can become part of your support network.

Here are my top tips for business success:
- ✓ Appoint an accountant from day one
- ✓ Follow the advice given to you in this book
- ✓ Create a weekly 'Action Planner' / 'To-Do List', to help keep track of those key tasks that need to be completed and make yourself accountable to completing them
- ✓ Network, Network, Network – It is amazing who you meet at networking events, get chatting to as many people as you can. Remember you don't know who they know that may want to buy your product/service
- ✓ Find a mentor who can help you on your business journey
- ✓ Stay positive and never give up

I wish you the best of luck with your business venture, and would love to hear about your business journey, especially if this book as helped you on your way. Please feel free to share your experiences with me at info@business-pod.co.uk.

A Practical Guide to Setting Up Your Business

Web: www.business-pod.co.uk

Email: - success@business-pod.co.uk

© 2016 The Business Pod Limited

www.ingramcontent.com/pod-product-compliance
Lightning Source LLC
Chambersburg PA
CBHW060404190526
45169CB00002B/751